INSPIRED PRAYERS

Praying the Scripture Promises that Motivated
Our Founding Fathers

BY DAVID KUBAL

**PrayerShop
Publishing**

Terre Haute, IN

PrayerShop Publishing is the publishing arm of Harvest Prayer Ministries and the Church Prayer Leaders Network. Harvest Prayer Ministries exists to transform lives through teaching prayer. Its online prayer store, www.prayershop.org, has more than 300 prayer resources available for purchase. We published this book in partnership with Intercessors for America.

Intercessors for America (IFA) informs, connects, and mobilizes a network of those who pray and fast for America. IFA provides Christians in churches and communities nationwide with information and tools to unite them in effective prayer.

Intercessors for America
Post Office Box 915
Purcellville, VA 20134
GetOutThePrayer.com - IFApray.org

ISBN: 978-1-935012-78-8

1 2 3 4 5 | 2021 2020 2019 2018 2017

TABLE OF CONTENTS

INTRODUCTION

I am often asked if I think God is finished with America. That question might prompt various responses, but ultimately, the answer is, "It depends." To be clear, it does not depend upon God, as though He would act in some odd, fickle way.

Scripture is very clear concerning nations that have become disobedient to Him. They may turn back in repentance (2 Chr. 7:14; Jer. 18:7; Ps. 95).

It also depends on the Church and prayer.

If believers will come before Him with desperate, humble prayers, relying on His mighty power to come to our nation, then I believe that God will restore America and continue to use our nation as a "city set on a hill" (Mt. 5:14).

We get the government we deserve! If Christians are disgruntled with our government, they need to look no further than the effectiveness of the Church stewarding our nation. Romans 13 reminds us that God is the one who sets authorities in place. It is the Church's job to cooperate with the hand of God through intercessory prayer and action to see God-fearing officials elected.

_~~\|/~~_

> *It is the Church's job to cooperate with the hand of God through intercessory prayer and action to see God-fearing officials elected.*

Many Christians across this nation are either turned off by politics or they don't see any hope. This is primarily because of four misunderstood principles in the Body of Christ today.

- Government is appointed by God for His purposes on the earth (Rom. 13:1).
- We need leaders who fear God (Ex. 18:21).
- Solutions come from God (Ps. 33:12).
- We must pray, "Your kingdom come. Your will be done on earth as it is in heaven" until Jesus returns (Mt. 6:10).

This is what we believe and what I hope the following chapters will clarify in a convincing way. Failure to understand and apply these principles has neutralized the Church into a state of inaction.

Will you pray with me through these four points, as we consider what God has for our nation? Greater spiritual results from the spreading of the Gospel message have come from the U.S. than from any other nation in the history of mankind. Let's not be the last generation to see this impact.

This resource is designed to guide those with a heart to pray for America. In *Inspired Prayers*, I will show the Scriptures that inspired our Founders to stake their lives to bring America into existence. I will then show how to apply these Scriptures in prayer as you seek God's purposes for the United States. I believe that the promises of Scripture that were important to them should be relied upon in our day as well!

CHAPTER ONE

DIVINE PURPOSE IN HUMAN GOVERNMENT

"The authorities that exist have been established by God."
(ROMANS 13:1)

uman government is God's idea and is His chosen way for mankind to steward His law. This stewardship (or governing) of His requirements is comparable to a fence around a flock of sheep, being both protective and restrictive. The fence provides safety for obedient sheep, but it is an unwanted restraint to the disobedient sheep looking to "go astray." Similarly, to a thief, the law is an impediment to evil when it commands, "You shall not steal" (with the implication of a penalty), while to the intended victim, the same edict serves to protect, *precisely because* it demands, "You shall not steal." Thus, human government represents God's divine order to keep man's sinfulness in check.

The Bible upholds the function of government, as in the following verse: "Let everyone be subject to the governing authorities, for there is no authority except that which God has established. The authorities that exist have been established by God" (Rom. 13:1).

However, when the godly do not shepherd government through intercession and action, human government, lacking divine guidance, fails to acknowledge God and loses its focus on truth. The result is an inability to define and maintain a moral worldview. When absolute standards are abandoned, all behavioral norms become relative, and there is no "right" or "wrong."

Long before the American colonies existed, John Calvin commented on Romans 13:4, which supports the necessity of the "magistrate" as God's minister to enforce the law as a consequence of man's sinfulness. In his *Institutes of the Christian Religion*, Calvin wrote:

> "'For he (the magistrate) is God's minister to us for good.' We understand from this, that [civil authority] is divinely appointed in order that we may be appointed by his power and protection against the malice and injustice of wicked men, and may lead peaceable and secure lives . . . but if it be in vain that he is given to us by the Lord for protection . . . it clearly follows that we may appeal to him and apply for his aid without any violation of piety." (*Institutes*, 4.20.4 to 4.20.19)

The nation's Founders understood this and applied it to the building of our nation. They knew their call from God was to construct a government based on biblical values. Remember, they grew up in an era that encompassed the peak of the First Great Awakening (circa 1740 to 1799). Their monumental works carried over into the Second Great Awakening, which provided a genuinely spiritual atmosphere in the growing American "experiment."

Thus, the Founders' lives developed in and were nurtured by two of the greatest evangelical revival periods in America's history. Although not all were evangelical Christians, they were pious men who acknowledged the Creator and were determined to recognize the "unalienable rights" that only a Divine Sovereign could bestow. They applied what they understood to create a very different government than that of England's Crown, which George Washington's army had fought to escape.

Further, they understood that God would grant them the government they deserved. It was with that unanimous sentiment that 56 men signed the Declaration of Independence. In the Declaration, they concluded with a united commitment: "And for the support of this Declaration, with a firm reliance on the protection of divine Providence, we mutually pledge to each other our Lives, our Fortunes and our sacred Honor."

Limited government is a biblical concept rooted in understanding man's sinfulness. The Scripture declares that "all have sinned and fall short of the glory of God" (Rom. 3:23). Apart from regeneration by the Holy Spirit, all are eternally condemned.

A biblical worldview incorporates this understanding. If, as Scripture teaches, man in his natural state is broken, it follows that society needs the Bible's influence in order to produce just standards. In and of itself, human government is incapable of creating a righteous social order. Rather, the influence of the Gospel must permeate the building process of a just society.

Jesus said, "It is not the healthy who need a doctor, but the sick. I have not come to call the righteous, but sinners" (Mk. 2:17). Stated differently, the Church cannot manipulate human nature to be moral. Lives must be changed from within. The role of government is to protect the citizenry and support that which is good, while providing an environment for its people to live in peace (see 1 Tim. 2:1-3). But in order for government to do good, those who serve must be capable of discerning good from evil and be motivated to choose what is right.

This requires spiritual foundations. A democratic republic can only be upheld by virtuous people.

—◦◦◦—

In order for government to do good, those who serve must be capable of discerning good from evil and be motivated to choose what is right.

This divinely instigated building of a nation with just and balanced government was designed to be stewarded with biblical standards. But in America, the rise of industry and technology birthed a human self-reliance that has no apparent need for God. As modern generations have become disengaged from the governing process, entrenched leaders tend to rule rather than to serve. We observe this today in our nation. America is clearly on a rapid decline into a swampland of moral and spiritual relativism, greed, compromise, and decay.

CHRISTIAN INFLUENCE

Christians have the potential of being the largest voting bloc in America! Together, we could sway elections through conscientious participation. We could influence our government by electing leaders with godly values. Yet, statistics show that fewer than half of evangelical believers are registered to vote, and half of those registered don't vote. Too many sit on the sidelines with no sense of duty to participate in government.

In summary, our federal government was designed to protect the people from exploitation and corrupt personal empowerment. The Founders gave us a government of laws. Boundaries were set, with checks and balances. Why? Because the original leaders didn't trust human nature, including their own. Have you wondered how they saw this so clearly?

A pastor-theologian from an earlier generation observed, "If George Washington was the father of our country, surely its 'grandfather' was John Calvin." To understand that, we must remember that the original goal of the Puritans (called "Separatists") was not the New World. The Mayflower first sailed in 1608 to Leyden, a village in Holland, where the group spent more than 10 years. Their purpose was to escape the Church of England, because they believed it was deviating from biblical teaching.

During that time, they were influenced by the Dutch Reformed Church, which had been built on strong Calvinism, the first principle of which was "(Man's) Total Depravity." This meant that human thought was never to be trusted to do good. Ultimately, the English "settlers" grew tired of the looser Dutch morality. They returned to England, reorganized, and set sail for America in 1620.

Because of this Puritan influence, some 150 years later, the Founders instinctively upheld limited government. The power of government had to be controlled. The most obvious way to set boundaries was to divide government into three equal branches: Legislative, Executive, and Judicial. This sectioning ensured the opportunity for representatives of the states and communities to make laws enforced through the courts. James Madison found a biblical basis for the three branches in Isa. 33:22: "For the LORD is our judge, the LORD is our lawgiver, the LORD is our king; it is he who will save us."

The Founders developed the U.S. Constitution, which seamlessly weaves together the twin understandings that the people's basic rights were gifts from the Creator and that balanced government would ensure those rights were not violated. When allowed to work, our

Constitution curbs the potential abuse of power that occurs when sinful man is involved. The Founders envisioned and lived for this. As a result, the U.S. Constitution is the longest standing document guiding any nation.

As you pray for our nation, thank God that He led the Founders to recognize His providence in creating a government to function for His purposes: to curb evil, to be an instrument in His hand, and to offer freedom of religious expression and the spread of the Gospel.

In order to survive, our nation needs leaders today with this viewpoint. The goal should be to reduce the role of government in America. At present, it is swollen and inefficient, stifling creativity, and virtually enslaving the people it was designed to serve and protect.

PRAY THE BIBLE PROMISES THAT INSPIRED OUR FOUNDING FATHERS

The Prayer in the First Congress, A.D. 1774. Courtesy of the Rector,
Church Wardens and Vestrymen of Christ Church, Philadelphia.

PRAYER POINTS:

DAY 1: Pray that more Christians would understand government is appointed by God for His purposes.

DAY 2: Pray that more Christians would understand our government's roots and give thanks to God for giving America its biblical foundations.

DAY 3: Pray that more Christians will recognize and—through prayer and participation—enthusiastically embrace all that God has appointed, including civil government.

DAY 4: Pray that in each election more Christians would register to vote, then study the issues, and vote wisely.

DAY 5: Pray that we seek to elect officials who understand the necessity of limited government.

✣ Scriptures to Pray ✣

- **1 TIMOTHY 2:1-2** – "I urge, then, first of all, that petitions, prayers, intercession and thanksgiving be made for all people—for kings and all those in authority, that we may live peaceful and quiet lives in all godliness and holiness."

- **ROMANS 13:1** – "Let everyone be subject to the governing authorities, for there is no authority except that which God has established. The authorities that exist have been established by God."

- **ISAIAH 33:22** – "For the LORD is our judge, the LORD is our lawgiver, the LORD is our king; it is he who will save us."

CHAPTER TWO

THE FEAR OF GOD

*"[Jehoshaphat] told them, 'Consider carefully what you do,
because you are not judging for mere mortals but for the LORD,
who is with you whenever you give a verdict. Now let the fear
of the LORD, be on you. Judge carefully, for with the LORD,
our God there is no injustice or partiality or bribery.'"*
(2 CHRONICLES 19:6-7)

A critical element of good government is the fear of God. A government that tries to lead without such recognition is like a ship without a rudder, having no ability to interpret right and wrong for its citizens or any providential purpose for that nation.

Our Founders understood this, as evidenced by Noah Webster's comment on elections:

> "When you become entitled to exercise the right of voting for public officers, let it be impressed on your mind that God commands you to choose for rulers, 'just men who will rule in the fear of God.' The preservation of government depends on the faithful discharge of this duty; if the citizens neglect their duty and place unprincipled men in office, the government will

soon be corrupted; laws will be made, not for the public good so much as for selfish or local purposes; corrupt or incompetent men will be appointed to execute the laws; the public revenues will be squandered on unworthy men; and the rights of the citizens will be violated or disregarded. If a republican government fails to secure public prosperity and happiness, it must be because the citizens neglect the divine commands, and elect bad men to make and administer the laws."

In referring to Exodus 18:21, Webster showed understanding of the lessons God taught Moses—to appoint leaders who understand their accountability to a Power higher than themselves. Any rulers, whether elected or appointed, who believe they answer only to peers or worse—to themselves—will quickly fail. We see this wherever dictators hold office only to enrich themselves at the expense of the people they initially swore to serve. Such nations are adrift from solid moorings.

It is important to understand the Old Testament concept of "the fear of the LORD," which has three different levels. The root word *yirah* is expressed as fleeing from pain, fearing God's punishment, and seeing correctly the awesomeness of God.

1. Fleeing from Pain: "It is a dreadful thing to fall into the hands of the living God" (Heb. 10:31).

2. Fearing God's Eternal Punishment: "And I saw the dead, great and small, standing before the throne, and books were opened. Another book was opened, which is the book of life. The dead were judged according to what they had done as recorded in the books" (Rev. 20:12).

3. Seeing Correctly God's Awesomeness: This gets to the heart of the meaning of "the fear of the LORD." The first two understandings of this "fear" are initial steps to salvation, indicating that through the

Gospel one first becomes cognizant of sin and eternal punishment but is not yet aware of the solution provided by God's grace.

A pastor from an earlier generation said, "The Gospel is bad news before it is good news," meaning that one must first understand "the wages of sin is death" before realizing "the gift of God is eternal life . . ." (Rom. 6:23). If we only become conscious of sin and learn that our guilt must result in a just penalty to be exacted by a righteous God, that knowledge alone brings condemnation. But when we "see correctly" that Jesus Christ provides redemption, and we receive God's promised forgiveness by faith, then the Gospel leads not to misery and the fear of death, but to a new relationship with God as a loving Father.

"The Gospel is bad news before it is good news." The "fear of the LORD" that results is a deep reverential and abiding trust. We want our stewardship of life to please Him. He alone deserves our worship, praise, and service.

This is beautifully linked in the Old Testament in a psalm of exultation:

> "He provided redemption for his people; he ordained his covenant forever—holy and awesome is his name. The fear of the LORD is the beginning of wisdom; all who follow his precepts have good understanding. To him belongs eternal praise." (Ps. 111:9-10)

Because of its importance, we should pray that leaders of our communities, states, and nation would find and embrace the fear of the Lord regardless of which level they come to understand: the fear of punishment in this life, the fear of punishment in the life to come, or by "seeing correctly God's awesomeness."

INFLUENCE OUR INTERCESSION

There are two approaches that should influence our intercession for America and its leaders with regard to the fear of God.

First, we can look at biblical precedents, where God sovereignly and directly confronted and called an individual to Himself for divine service, resulting in a "fear-of-the-LORD" response. Examples abound, such as Nebuchadnezzar, whose dream, with Daniel's interpretation, gave so much light to future events; Queen Esther, who risked a sovereign king's wrath by interceding for the Jewish people's deliverance from extermination; and Saul of Tarsus, who encountered the risen Christ on the road to Damascus. Can such experiences still occur? Undoubtedly, yes; and we are free to pray, "Lord, please do it again!"

More likely, however, an alternate approach will reveal God's purposes through His people. We must patiently intercede for widespread revival through a repentant and awakened Church. Then, as transformed communities of believers present a confident, triumphant witness that God changes lives through the Gospel, many, including political leaders, will be radically saved and will become aware of the fear of the Lord.

At critical moments in the establishment of our nation, godly leaders called us to understand the importance of this. We can learn much by reading the words they proclaimed on the first *National Day of Humiliation, Fasting, and Prayer*, called for July 20, 1775:

". . . that we may, with united hearts and voices, unfeignedly
confess and deplore our many sins; and offer up our joint sup-
plications to the all-wise, omnipotent, and merciful Disposer
of all events; humbly beseeching him to forgive our iniquities,
to remove our present calamities, to avert those desolating
judgments, with which we are threatened. . . ."[1]

While the words, "the fear of God," do not appear in this relatively
brief Proclamation, the spirit of worship and surrender to the One
they referred to as "the great Governor of the World" is evident in
every phrase.

In the present moment, one needs only to engage the news media
to acknowledge that "fear" is rampant in today's world. It attacks
everyone, but it is up to each person to choose what or whom will be
feared—our circumstances or God. If the choice is to fear God, our
perspective changes, as the fear of the Lord overcomes every other fear,
and we find a resting place in His grace. Isaiah's prophecy still brings
reassurance today:

"So do not fear, for I am with you; do not be dismayed, for
I am your God. I will strengthen you and help you; I will
uphold you with my righteous right hand." (Isa. 41:10)

As we pray for leaders to discover and experience the fear of God,
we should not live in fear of circumstances. Let us recognize the necessity for each of us to intercede for our country in the fear of the Lord.
God will strengthen us and uphold the righteous causes for which we
are praying.

PRAY THE BIBLE PROMISES THAT INSPIRED OUR FOUNDING FATHERS

The Prayer in the First Congress, A.D. 1774. Courtesy of the Rector, Church Wardens and Vestrymen of Christ Church, Philadelphia.

PRAYER POINTS:

DAY 1: Give thanks and pray for your political leaders—local, state, and national—who lead with a fear of the Lord.

DAY 2: Pray for the Church to awaken to a renewed focus on the fear of the Lord.

DAY 3: Pray that pastors would be free from the fear of man and preach the fear of the Lord.

DAY 4: Pray that our leaders would be convicted to "see correctly" the awesomeness of God and our Savior, Jesus Christ.

DAY 5: Pray that the fear of the Lord would overtake any fear of circumstances.

✢ *Scriptures to Pray* ✣

- **2 CHRONICLES 19:6-7** – "[Jehoshaphat] told them, 'Consider carefully what you do, because you are not judging for mere mortals but for the LORD who is with you whenever you give a verdict. Now let the fear of the LORD be on you. Judge carefully, for with the LORD our God there is no injustice or partiality or bribery.'"
- **EXODUS 18:21** – "But select capable men from all the people—men who fear God, trustworthy men who hate dishonest gain—and appoint them as officials over thousands, hundreds, fifties and tens."
- **PSALMS 111:9-10** – "He provided redemption for his people; he ordained his covenant forever—holy and awesome is his name. The fear of the LORD is the beginning of wisdom; all who follow his precepts have good understanding. To him belongs eternal praise."

ENDNOTES:

[1]To read the 1775 Proclamation in its entirety, go to http://biblescripture. net/National.html, where it is preceded by a brief introduction noting the recognition of Almighty God and a kind response even to King George. Hostilities with England had just begun in Lexington and Concord (Massachusetts), and in 1775, the framers of this Proclamation felt that outright war could be avoided.

A year later, the 1776 Proclamation takes a more adversarial tone, yet shows the Founders and their fellow leaders still worshipful of God, repentant, and recognizing His providence and blessing in all the affairs of the young colonies, even as independence was declared and the Revolution proceeded. These were pious men who knew the fear of God and lived by its implications.

CHAPTER THREE

AN APPEAL TO HEAVEN

"Surely his salvation is near those who fear him,
that his glory may dwell in our land."

(PSALM 85:9)

By all logic and reasonable analysis, the United States of America should not exist. Given the many reasons for our nation to have crumbled—indeed, not ever to have gotten underway—we should not be enjoying the freedoms that we have. So, what made the difference?

The broad answer is, of course, God's providential purposes. But as to the means used, our country was founded by leaders who appealed to heaven. Nations have come and gone or exist in one form or another without the grace given to our Founders. But America's origins were steeped in the fear of God. Its foundations were derived from biblical truth centered in recognition of God as Supreme Ruler of Nations. There has never been a constitutional republic formed and launched with the promise and hope given to our land of freedom—never in the history of mankind. So we may ask, "How did such an 'impossible' phenomenon occur?"

There has never been a constitutional republic formed and launched with the promise and hope given to our land of freedom.

We may begin by looking to history. As God began stirring the hearts of philosophers in the 17th century (setting foundations for the later so-called "Enlightenment"), John Locke (1632–1704) was among a small contingent of British thinkers who rejected the theory of the "divine right of kings," which was the prevailing belief until the end of the 17th century. Judges 11 was the impetus behind the thought that God must be relied upon for the solutions of a nation's problems.

Judges 11 tells of the account of Jephthah, a warrior in Israel who later became one of its judges. When Israel was threatened by the King of Ammon, Jephthah was dragged into this war against his will by his leaders. Those very leaders had denounced him and made him leave the country just before this threat. However, God's calling on his life came full circle and, recognizing him as a man of valor, they called him back to lead the army. Jephthah could have chosen to be bitter at a government that had rejected him, but he knew the heart of God was for Israel to prevail.

He first tried to negotiate with the King of Ammon, but when that failed, Jephthah prepared for action and eventual victory by depending on God and praying:

> "Let the LORD, the Judge, decide the dispute this day between the Israelites and the Ammonites." (Judg. 11:27)

Locke, in *The Second Treatise on Civil Government* (published in 1690), referred to this passage as he wrote:

"Had there been any such court, any superior jurisdiction on earth, to determine the right between Jephtha and the Ammonites, they had never come to a state of war: but we see he was forced to appeal to heaven. The Lord the Judge (says he) be judge this day between the children of Israel and the children of Ammon (Judg. 11: 27), and then prosecuting, and relying on his appeal, he leads out his army to battle: and therefore in such controversies, where the question is put, who shall be judge? It cannot be meant, who shall decide the controversy; everyone knows what Jephtha here tells us, that the Lord the Judge shall judge. Where there is no judge on earth, the appeal lies to God in heaven. That question then cannot mean, who shall judge, whether another hath put himself in a state of war with me, and whether I may, as Jephtha did, appeal to heaven in it? "Of that I myself can only be judge in my own conscience, as I will answer it, at the great day, to the supreme judge of all men."[1]

This Old Testament example of appealing to the Lord, our Judge, was relied upon by many of our Founding Fathers, including George Washington, who, as the leader of the Continental Army, purchased ships that were converted into warships destined to protect Boston Harbor from the British supply ships. This ragtag bunch of sailors with converted merchant ships—some paid for personally by Washington himself—knew their hope of success was in God. The flag they flew reflected this dependence. On it was written, "An Appeal to Heaven." This was the first flag flown over the U.S. Navy, as Congress legislated it into existence in October 1775. In many ways, it became the first unofficial flag of the Revolution and was the army's battle cry.

OUR FIRST FLAG

A picture of a pine tree appears on the "An Appeal to Heaven" flag. The origin of this symbol goes back to 1691 and the "broad-arrow policy." As the pilgrims arrived in the New World, their storm-battered ships required refurbishing, and to accomplish this, white pine trees were harvested to provide straight masts for their ships. The British parliament passed legislation requiring the pilgrims to use trees less than 150 feet tall, leaving the larger trees for the Empire's navy. These trees would be marked with the symbol of a broad arrow.

The restrictions put upon the settlers was a point of great tension, which resulted in the Pine Tree Rebellion of 1772, a rebellion similar to the Boston Tea Party of 1773. The image of the white pine became a reminder to the colonists of their fight against an unjust king.

This appeal to heaven, as evidenced by the pine tree flag, was recognition of the colonists' only hope and was reflected in the Declaration of Independence wording:

> "We, therefore, the Representatives of the United States of America, in General Congress, Assembled, appealing to the Supreme Judge of the world for the rectitude of our intentions, do, in the Name, and by Authority of the good People of these Colonies, solemnly publish and declare, That these United Colonies are, and of Right ought to be Free and Independent States."

The battles facing our nation today are different from and more complex than the battles of the Founders. When we consider our issues—the national debt, threats of terrorism, legal abortion on demand, and many others—we know it will be much more difficult to find solutions. Our only hope is to appeal to heaven.

We need to pray first, then seek to elect leaders who recognize the need for divine wisdom to fix the issues that can only be solved through righteous and just legislation. We must also pray for leaders who are humble and open to solutions that come from sources outside themselves. This is consistent with our previous call for men and women to lead in the "fear of the Lord."

God's glorious intervention through the lives of our Founding Fathers will never be repeated, enviable though it is. It was unique in human history. God's heart is always to do a fresh work—first in, and then through—His Church, so we can pray with the psalmist:

> "Will you not revive us again, that your people may rejoice in you? . . . that [God's] glory may dwell in our land." (Ps. 85:6, 9)

We need to pray for leaders who would be used of God for this purpose. Patrick Henry said it well:

> "There is a just God who presides over the destinies of nations, and who will raise up friends to fight our battles for us."

We need to pray that every good purpose that God has ordained for the future and destiny of this nation will be accomplished. From relying on Scripture, intercessors have no doubt about what God can do—that is, what He is able to accomplish through His infinite power. But they also know what God will do and does do is most often the result of His people's fervent and believing prayer.

PRAY THE BIBLE PROMISES THAT INSPIRED OUR FOUNDING FATHERS

The Prayer in the First Congress, A.D. 1774. Courtesy of the Rector, Church Wardens and Vestrymen of Christ Church, Philadelphia.

PRAYER POINTS:

DAY 1: Pray for leaders who recognize the need for divine wisdom.

DAY 2: Pray that Christians will awaken to their authority in faithful intercession.

DAY 3: Pray that the Church will find unity in crying out to God.

DAY 4: Pray that in crying out to God, there will be a concerted "appeal to heaven" for God's solutions.

DAY 5: Pray that the Lord will revive our nation as we appeal to Him.

✷ *Scriptures to Pray* ✷

- **PSALMS 85:6** — "Will you not revive us again, that your people may rejoice in you?"
- **JUDGES 11:27** — "Let the LORD, the Judge, decide the dispute of this day between the Israelites and the Ammonites."
- **PSALMS 85:9** — "Surely his salvation is near those who fear him . . . that his glory may dwell in our land."

ENDNOTES:

[1]John Locke developed and wrote the philosophy that there was no legitimate government under the "divine right of kings" theory. This theory asserted that God chose some people to rule on earth in His will. Therefore, whatever the monarch decided had to be the will of God. When you criticized the ruler, you were, in effect, challenging God. This was a very powerful philosophy for the existing ruler. Locke's writings challenged that view.

It is widely believed that the reason Locke's writings influenced the framers of the United States Constitution was his notion that the power to govern was obtained from the permission of the people. This view very much appealed to Jefferson, Adams, and Patrick Henry. Further, Locke thought that the purpose of government was to protect the natural rights of its citizens. He said that natural rights were life, liberty, and property, and that all people automatically earned these simply by being born. If or when a government did not protect those rights, the citizens had the right to overthrow the government.

CHAPTER FOUR

MAY YOUR KINGDOM COME!

"In this manner, therefore, pray: Our Father in heaven,
hallowed be Your name. Your kingdom come.
Your will be done on earth as it is in heaven."
(MATTHEW 6:9-10 NKJV)

When Jesus taught His disciples to pray, He gave them a very simple prayer that most professing Christians can quote. Yet it seems few people realize the full implications of the first request we are instructed to pray: May Your kingdom come, O Lord, with the same power and comprehensive effects Your rule has in heaven. As we pray, the question in many Christians' minds may be, "Yes, we want God's kingdom, but what does it look like?"

The question is important and best understood if we realize that the manifestation of God's kingdom on earth has two distinct phases. Before these kingdom principles can be expressed through God's people, they must first be at work in us.

Throughout the Gospels, our Lord's attention was on personal application. Only later would the broader meaning of "Your kingdom come" be fully revealed. We must remember that the "model prayer" was given twice, almost verbatim, in two different settings (Mt. 6:9-13 and Lk. 11:2-4). Matthew has recorded Jesus' early teaching, where the application was on humility and forgiveness. In Luke's account, one of the disciples asked Jesus, "Lord, teach us to pray." The follow-up emphasis was to trust in God's provision and pray persistently, as in, "Then Jesus said to them, 'Suppose you have a friend, and you go to him at midnight and say, "Friend, lend me three loaves of bread . . ."'"(Lk. 11:5).

Both emphases—the necessity to forgive (Matthew) and persistent intercession based on God's faithfulness (Luke)—are vitally important spiritual attainments for Christ's disciples before an effective kingdom message can be delivered to the world. The larger kingdom expression is coming, but first God will do a deep awakening in His Church.

Note how Jesus began His ministry: "From that time on Jesus began to preach, 'Repent, for the kingdom of heaven has come near'" (Mt. 4:17). And while some believed, many more did not, as confirmed in John's account: "He came to His own, and His own did not receive Him" (Jn. 1:11 NKJV).

Again, Jesus' focus was on personal needs and individual responses. He answered one questioner by saying, "You are not far from the kingdom of God" (Mk. 12:34). His directive to His disciples was "seek first the kingdom of God" (Mt. 6:33 NKJV). With kingdom pursuit first, other needs would be supplied.

Jesus made this clear when He was questioned by the religious leaders of His day:

> "Now when He was asked by the Pharisees when the kingdom of God would come, He answered them and said, 'The kingdom of God does not come with observation; nor will they say, 'See here!' or 'See there!' For indeed, the kingdom of God is within you." (Lk. 17:20-21 NKJV)

The two-sided aspect of the kingdom explains the answer Jesus gave Pilate on the eve of His crucifixion. "Jesus said, 'My kingdom is not of this world. If it were, my servants would fight to prevent my arrest by the Jewish leaders. But now my kingdom is from another place'" (Jn. 18:36).

Finally, after His resurrection, Jesus "appeared to them . . . and spoke about the kingdom of God," which prompted their question prior to His ascension: "Lord, are you at this time going to restore the kingdom to Israel?" (Acts 1:3, 6-7). His answer may have shocked them, but everything hung in the balance, because this tiny, fledgling Church was destined to grow and carry the "Gospel of the kingdom" to all the world and to every generation.

> "He said to them: 'It is not for you to know the times or dates the Father has set by his own authority. But you will receive power when the Holy Spirit comes on you; and you will be my witnesses in Jerusalem, and in all Judea and Samaria, and to the ends of the earth.'" (Acts 1:7-8)

In heaven, God rules with power and love that encompasses all activity. His kingdom will one day be manifest in all nations, when that which is important to God will be important to each citizen who embraces His will; where His government will have no end; and where there will be a holy fear of the Almighty, resulting in the King's values expressed continuously.

May His kingdom come on earth, as it is in heaven! This should continue to be our petition, as it was in America's earliest days.

*May His kingdom come on earth, as it is in
heaven! This should continue to be our petition,
as it was in America's earliest days.*

Prayer was not a foreign thought to the Founders of our nation.
Samuel Adams, as governor of Massachusetts, called his state to a day
of fasting and prayer on March 20, 1797, with the following words:

> "I concede that we cannot better express ourselves than by
> humbly supplicating the Supreme Ruler of the world— that
> wars may cease in all the Earth, and that the confusions that
> are and have been among the Nations may be overruled for
> the promoting and speedily bringing on the holy and happy
> period when the kingdom of our Lord and Saviour Jesus Christ
> may be everywhere established, and all the people willingly
> bow to the Sceptre of Him who is the Prince of Peace."

John Hancock declared three days of thanksgiving and fasting,
invoking the God of this universe to establish His kingdom

> ". . . that the spiritual kingdom of our Lord and Savior Jesus
> Christ may be continually increasing until the whole earth
> shall be filled with His glory . . ." (Oct. 29, 1788).

> ". . . that He would finally overrule all events to the advance-
> ment of the Redeemer's kingdom and the establishment of
> universal peace and good will among men . . ." (Feb. 24, 1792).

". . . that the kingdom of our Lord and Savior Jesus Christ may be established in peace and righteousness among all the nations of the earth . . ." (Oct. 25, 1792).

These words from our Founding Fathers have ringing in the background the powerful, prophetic words of Isaiah describing and declaring the rule and reign of Jesus Christ:

> "For to us a child is born, to us a Son is given, and the government will be on his shoulders. And he will be called Wonderful Counselor, Mighty God, Everlasting Father, Prince of Peace. Of the greatness of his government and peace there will be no end. He will reign on David's throne and over his kingdom, establishing and upholding it with justice and righteousness from that time on and forever. The zeal of the LORD Almighty will accomplish this." (Isa. 9:6-7)

This ultimate expression of God's kingdom will honor our Savior, Jesus Christ. The government will be on His shoulders. His submission to His Father gives Him the right to the throne. The role of His Church is to cooperate with God through prayer and intercession. In that day, all kings and leaders will be instruments to accomplish His purposes. There are biblical examples of unwitting rulers being used of God, such as Cyrus (Isa. 45). Let us pray for more elected officials whom God will use to establish His will in our day.

KINGDOM FULLY REVEALED

When God's kingdom is fully revealed, people will recognize His authority, and be in awe of His ability and power. The ruler of this ultimate kingdom will be a "Wonderful Counselor," revered by all. Every knee will bow to Him, willingly or not. He will rule in love or, as Psalm 2:9 declares, ". . . with a rod of iron." His kingdom will demonstrate not only the power of divine love, as from a kind, eternal Father, but also, where necessary, the justice of His judgment. The Bible describes the Father's love as quick to forgive where there is repentance.

As we look at governments and nations today, we see partisanship, bickering, and disunity. When God's kingdom is established, the most distinguishing feature will be peace. No more striving and contention, but perfect and abiding peace.

Jesus Christ will rule in righteousness and with justice. He will always do what is right. And all of this will be accomplished by the "zeal of the Lord Almighty," through a revived, triumphant Church.

Let us continue to pray the very first request that our Lord Jesus instructed us to pray: "Your kingdom come. Your will be done, on earth as it is in heaven."

PRAY THE BIBLE PROMISES THAT INSPIRED OUR FOUNDING FATHERS

The Prayer in the First Congress, A.D. 1774. Courtesy of the Rector, Church Wardens and Vestrymen of Christ Church, Philadelphia.

PRAYER POINTS:

DAY 1: Pray that our elected officials would cooperate with the establishment of God's kingdom on this earth.

DAY 2: Pray that the Church will awaken to the hope of seeing God's kingdom established on earth.

DAY 3: Pray that Americans would elect God-fearing leaders who will call the citizenry to fasting and supplication.

DAY 4: Pray that revival in the Church will bring down walls of division and result in unity.

DAY 5: Pray for our government to recognize freedom of conscience for Christian ministries and businesses.

✻ *Scriptures to Pray* ✻

- **MATTHEW 6:9-10** — "In this manner, therefore, pray: Our Father in heaven, hallowed be Your name. Your kingdom come. Your will be done on earth as it is in heaven."

- **MATTHEW 4:17** — "From that time on Jesus began to preach, 'Repent, for the kingdom of heaven has come near.'"

- **ISAIAH 9:6-7** — "For to us a child is born, to us a Son is given, and the government will be on his shoulders. And he will be called Wonderful Counselor, Mighty God, Everlasting Father, Prince of Peace. Of the greatness of his government and peace there will be no end. He will reign on David's throne and over his kingdom,

establishing and upholding it with justice and righteousness from that time on and forever. The zeal of the
LORD Almighty will accomplish this."

CHAPTER FIVE

SELF-GOVERNMENT

"The name of the LORD is a strong tower;
the righteous run to it and are safe."
(PROVERBS 18:10, NKJV)

Self-government is the bedrock of our nation. The New World frontier—later, to become the United States of America—was founded by people seeking freedom: freedom to worship as conscience directed and to conduct their lives the way they chose. Their attitudes about freedom were formed by history and personal experience of dealing with oppressive rulers and restrictive governments. In short, the Founders of the United States were determined to govern themselves.

In order to experience this freedom, our Founders understood the necessity that individuals be allowed to make moral and virtuous decisions.

"Only a virtuous people are capable of freedom. As nations become corrupt and vicious, they have more need of masters." (Benjamin Franklin, 1787)

"The Scriptures tell us righteousness exalteth a Nation." (Abigail Adams)

"The only foundation for . . . a republic is to be laid in Religion. Without this there can be no virtue, and without virtue there can be no liberty, and liberty is the object and life of all republican governments." (Benjamin Rush)

"Our Constitution was made only for a moral and religious people. It is wholly inadequate to the government of any other." (John Adams)

Without virtuous, self-governing people, evil thinking will eventually corrupt human government. Selfishness, greed, and debauchery would enter the culture, resulting in the degradation of that society and turning it into a collection of corrupt individuals with ". . . every man doing whatever is right in his own eyes . . ." (Deut. 12:8 NKJV). God has woven this principle into mankind, declaring that His ways are highest and best, and that without His enablement, human understanding could never comprehend or emulate divine wisdom.

To demonstrate His ideal plan, God placed a perfect man (that is, one who had never sinned) in a perfect environment and gave that individual and his equally perfect wife a very simple test. He did not give multiple commandments—only one. In that moral perfection, God built into them the choice to obey or disobey. And there, in a perfect environment, with no innate "sin nature" and with full provision for their happiness, they chose to disobey and to eat fruit from the only tree that was forbidden. This proved that man on his own—without divine intervention—cannot and will not find within himself the instinct or ability to fulfill God's requirements or to produce a just society that reflects His glory and fulfills His purpose.

A CRITICAL QUESTION

That brings us to a critical question: Where do we find morality? Our Founders wanted to believe that morality and natural law have been revealed to us. This is what was meant when the Declaration of Independence referred to "Laws of Nature and Nature's God." They believed that because only God can define morality, only He can make just laws. Government leaders can—at best—try to formulate laws that reflect God's standard of justice.

In this quest, the Founders invoked the writings of William Blackstone, one of the most influential legal minds in history and the father of British Common Law. Blackstone wrote:

> "The doctrines . . . delivered [by an immediate and direct revelation] we call the revealed or divine law, and they are to be found only in the Holy Scriptures. . . . Upon these two foundations, the law of nature and the law of revelation, depend all human laws; that is to say, no human laws should be suffered to contradict these."[1]

Therefore, the education and training of "moral people" to excel in self-government was central to our Founders' understanding of how a republic would best operate and endure. Most early New England colleges (today, the "Ivy League"), were chartered to train ministers and aid students in understanding the Scriptures, including the necessity of personal salvation. Note this lofty passage from Harvard College's original *Handbook for Students:*

Most early New England colleges (today, the "Ivy League"), were chartered to train ministers.

"Let every student be plainly instructed and earnestly pressed to consider well: the main end of his life and studies is 'to know God and Jesus Christ, which is eternal life' (John 17.3), and therefore to lay Christ in the bottom, as the only foundation of all sound knowledge and learning. And seeing the Lord only giveth wisdom, let everyone seriously set himself by prayer in secret to seek it of Him (Prov. 2:6)."

Calling on God for wisdom and understanding, seeking Him more than treasure, holding to a deep understanding of the need to fear the Almighty—these were basic tenets within the worldview of those who founded our country. This provided an environment where men and women strove to be virtuous people, pursuing personal holiness, which was understood to be crucial, not only for a life pleasing to God, but also a life worthy of a patriot in helping to settle the new country and provide a network of just laws to guide a growing society.

When a country rejects these ideals, and leaders define law independently, thereby altering the nation's direction, the tendency of those in authority is to create dependency by providing its citizens' every need. This moves such people toward socialism and, eventually, to full-blown Marxism. As government grows, building greater dependency on itself, the citizens will of necessity, rely on government and not on God. The result is a gradual loss of skills and self-reliance. The government then takes the place of God. The society first becomes secular and eventually atheistic. Such descent is inevitable.

We see this trend in modern Europe, where once-beautiful cathedrals have become museums devoid of God's Presence. Similarly, our own nation has sunk to a place where a robust God-consciousness of half a century ago has drifted into a state of outright antagonism toward spiritual values.

Only when a nation governs itself with reliance on God rather than "Big Brother's" largesse will it have opportunity to remain a healthy society. Scripture clearly proclaims the need for divine supremacy in government. For example, "Blessed is the nation whose God is the LORD" (Ps. 33:12), and "Righteousness exalts a nation, but sin is a reproach to any people" (Prov. 14:34, NKJV).

Israel's Old Testament history is a sad story of spiritual ups and downs. Their lives mirrored each successive reigning king. If he was obedient to God's laws, the people flourished; if he worshiped idols, so did they. What a vivid example of the need for godly leaders!

As the First Continental Congress gathered to offer an opening prayer, they dedicated the fledgling nation to the Lord with the following excerpt from Rev. Jacob Duché, a local, godly minister:

> "Lord, our Heavenly Father, high and mighty King of Kings, and Lord of Lords, who dost from Thy throne behold all the dwellers on earth, and reignest with power supreme and uncontrolled over all the kingdoms, empires and governments; look down in mercy we beseech Thee, on these American States, who have fled to Thee from the rod of the oppressor, and thrown themselves on Thy gracious protection, desiring henceforth to be dependent only on Thee. . . . All this we ask in the name and through the merits of Jesus Christ, Thy Son, Our Savior. Amen." (First Prayer in Congress, September 7, 1774, Carpenters' Hall, Philadelphia, PA)

PRAY THE BIBLE PROMISES THAT INSPIRED OUR FOUNDING FATHERS

The Prayer in the First Congress, A.D. 1774. Courtesy of the Rector,
Church Wardens and Vestrymen of Christ Church, Philadelphia.

PRAYER POINTS:

DAY 1: Pray for the election of leaders who have not strayed from faith in God.

DAY 2: Pray for the emergence of leaders who honor the principles of the Bible.

DAY 3: Pray for leaders who want increased self-government and less central government.

DAY 4: Pray for leaders who believe and live the Gospel while pursuing personal holiness.

DAY 5: Pray for God's compassionate conviction on fellow Christians who have not yet decided to use their right to vote, that they will embrace this God-ordained duty.

✠ *Scriptures to Pray* ✠

- **PROVERBS 18:10** – "The name of the LORD is a strong tower; the righteous run to it and are safe." (NKJV)
- **PSALMS 33:12** – "Blessed is the nation whose God is the LORD."
- **PROVERBS 14:34** – "Righteousness exalts a nation, but sin is a reproach to any people." (NKJV)

ENDNOTES:

[1]William Blackstone, *Commentaries on the Laws of England*, Introduction, pages 42-43.

While it is beyond the scope of these devotional studies, readers would be rewarded to learn more of the life and legal contributions of Sir William Blackstone (1723–1780). In God's providence, this self-taught, mostly sickly, often-mediocre British lawyer became—through two series of lectures at Oxford University, which formed the basic text of his four-volume *Commentaries*–one of the most widely quoted and relied-on legal minds in English history for 100 years. Blackstone's influence in America came through publication of his work in Philadelphia and "discovery" by Benjamin Franklin (and others), and thus to the framers of our foundational documents, primarily due to his concept of "natural law." In American history, his logic and legal reasoning are revered. He understood and relied on divine revelation, having strong faith that "the Holy Scriptures" were, indeed, the Word of God and the only basis for orderly self-government. Thomas Jefferson took Blackstone's "the law of nature and the law of revelation" and turned it into the "Laws of Nature and Nature's God." Historically, William Blackstone is an example of God's providential use of an outsider's influence in the development of both our Declaration of Independence and the U.S. Constitution. Blackstone's secure place as a "distant founder" of our nation's basic documents and attitudes toward forming and upholding the laws of the land can hardly be overstated.

CHAPTER SIX

MORALITY IN HUMAN GOVERNMENT

"The belief in a God All Powerful,
wise and good, is so essential to the moral order of the
World and to the happiness of man."
–JAMES MADISON

These are the wise words of James Madison, fourth president of the United States, who is considered by many historians to be "the father of the Constitution," including the Bill of Rights. Morality is a critical component of a free society. It demands principles that determine what is right and what is wrong. Essentially, it defines the character of any culture. A society without moral values based on absolute truth would be one of intolerable chaos, where every person behaves by his own standards, and leaders guide with flawed thinking. John Adams expressed it this way:

"We have no government armed with power capable of contending with human passions unbridled by morality and religion. Avarice, ambition, revenge or gallantry would break the strongest cords of our Constitution as a whale goes through a net. Our Constitution was made only for a moral and religious people. It is wholly inadequate to the government of any other."

To some degree, the ability to discern moral matters comes from natural law, a vital concept the Founders of our nation understood. Natural law is an unchanging body of principles written into human conscience by the Creator, who gives mankind the innate, though limited, ability to understand His law. The Bible confirms this more than once. For example, note the Apostle Paul's argument:

"For since the creation of the world God's invisible qualities—his eternal power and divine nature—have been clearly seen, being understood from what has been made, so that people are without excuse." (Rom. 1:20)

And once again, in the very next chapter:

"Indeed, when Gentiles, who do not have the law, do by nature things required by the law, they are a law for themselves, even though they do not have the law. They show that the requirements of the law are written on their hearts, their consciences also bearing witness . . ." (Rom. 2:14-15)

The human conscience, built into man's spirit by the Creator, gives some enablement to act morally, even without a regenerated spirit. No one is devoid of some sense of right and wrong. We also know that it is possible to harden our hearts or sear the conscience by repeated disregard for truth, making it impossible for the natural mind to respond correctly. But when a life is regenerated by the Holy

Spirit through the power of the Gospel, one is free from the law's condemnation and finds a peaceful relationship with God as Father (Rom. 5:1). Having a personal knowledge of Christ through faith provides a "heart of flesh," generating within the Christian a desire to surrender and obey.

As new believers encounter God's Word, they discover that the fear of the Lord is at the foundational level of morality. This is the understanding that everyone is accountable to God as the Supreme Ruler of the universe. For a nation to build morality into its ethos, it must have leaders who recognize their accountability to God. This is largely absent in America in the 21st century political climate. This absence blinds people from handling moral issues appropriately. The fear of the Lord brings alignment to a person's life, resulting in divine order. Multiply that result by many individuals, and a community—perhaps even a nation—can be addressed for moral adjustment.

> *For a nation to build morality into its ethos,*
> *it must have leaders who recognize their*
> *accountability to God.*

King Solomon, with all his riches, power, and early wisdom, acquired this insight toward the end of his reign when he wrote:

> "Everything is meaningless . . . here is the conclusion of the matter: Fear God and keep his commandments, for this is the duty of all mankind." (Eccl. 12:8, 13)

Sadly, Solomon squandered much of God's blessing through wrong choices, but he learned from his mistakes. This offers hope that people can be changed, which the New Testament confirms. Through the Gospel, God gives new life that reflects both His character and His nature. In New Testament language, this involves "the renewing of [the] mind" (Rom. 12:2). This is preceded by regeneration, which illuminates and frees the conscience through faith in Jesus Christ.

But conscience and awareness of natural law do not alone guarantee lawful or chaste behavior. Saul of Tarsus, for example, had an understanding of natural law and much more. He was educated in the Mosaic law and had an intense zeal motivated by an active, though misdirected, conscience. He believed it was God's will to persecute the followers of Jesus. His goal was to destroy the fledgling Church.

In Saul, we see no lack of conscientious dedication to his terrorist-like goals. The problem was that he was blinded by sin, having a deranged sense of right and wrong. He didn't need re-education; he needed to be saved and then redirected by the Spirit of God.

This demonstrates a truth the intercessor must remember. A candidate or elected official possessing the right pedigree or political backing does not equal a readiness to lead. He or she still needs a sense of accountability to the divine standard to change a deficient perspective. We must never lose heart, but at all times pray the promises of Scripture such as this: "The Lord confides in those who fear him; he makes his covenant known to them" (Ps. 25:14).

Morality is further encouraged through upholding religious freedom, reading the Scripture, and humble pursuit of God. Our nation will be at its best when we honor a strong sense of morality based in the fear and reverence of God. Self-government is possible, because God has given mankind the ability to understand right and wrong. But with understanding must come the inner spiritual impetus to choose between the two. That involves having a strong moral compass aligned with truth.

A BLESSED COUNTRY

No country in the history of the world has been blessed more than the United States. No other country has had the opportunity to experience the levels of freedom that we have enjoyed. No country has enjoyed citizen participation in the political process as fully as have Americans. The future has promise to us who believe that God's ways and God's laws can and should be recognized and honored through human government. We best serve our country and its leaders by praying for them. As we intercede, we must also wield our voting privilege for the candidates we believe are morally upright, best represent biblical morality, and, at least outwardly, exhibit the fear of the Lord to some degree.

As we pray for present and future leaders of our country, we might well recall the words of John Jay, the first Chief Justice of the U.S. Supreme Court; "Providence has given our people the choice of their rulers, and it is the duty, as well as privilege and interest, of a Christian nation to select and prefer Christians for their rulers." Today, we prefer the word "leaders" rather than "rulers," but Chief Justice Jay made a good point.

While reflecting on our privilege of voting for leaders, let us not forget that the gift also includes accountability. Since God has called our nation into being and given His people the responsibility to steward it through prayer and action, we must pray and we must vote. In addition, we must pray that our friends, including those who sit near us Sunday morning in our various church services, will also pray and vote.

Benjamin Franklin wrote, ". . . only a virtuous people are capable of freedom. As nations become corrupt and vicious, they have more need of masters."

This is a picture of our country at present. In God's providence, the corruption of our initial freedoms is not complete, as there are many in both the Church and in government service who have not bowed their knees to the false gods of materialism, moral decay, immorality, or greed. As we pray over this subject of morality, let us intercede diligently and fervently for revival to come to the Church.

PRAY THE BIBLE PROMISES THAT INSPIRED OUR FOUNDING FATHERS

The Prayer in the First Congress, A.D. 1774. Courtesy of the Rector, Church Wardens and Vestrymen of Christ Church, Philadelphia.

PRAYER POINTS:

DAY 1: Pray for God to raise up leaders who will guide our country to become a moral nation.

DAY 2: Pray for an awakened Church to support pastors and leaders who speak and teach truth without compromise.

DAY 3: Pray that our leaders will recognize "days of prayer, repentance, and fasting" for God's mercy and grace.

DAY 4: Pray for God to raise up leaders in the Church and government who are unabashedly Christian and who will encourage prayer and reading of the Bible in our homes and in our schools.

DAY 5: Pray for revival that will result in a new respect for moral law and the value of life in the womb.

⚡ *Scriptures to Pray* ⚡

- **ROMANS 2:12-15** — "Indeed, when Gentiles, who do not have the law, do by nature things required by the law, they are a law for themselves, even though they do not have the law. They show that the requirements of the law are written on their hearts, their consciences also bearing witness . . ."
- **ECCLESIASTES 12:13** — "Now all has been heard; here is the conclusion of the matter: Fear God and keep his commandments, for this is the whole duty of man."
- **PSALMS 25:14** — "The LORD confides in those who fear him; he makes his covenant known to them."

CHAPTER SEVEN

FREEDOM OF RELIGION

"Blessed is the nation whose God is the Lord . . ."
(PSALM 33:12)

Freedom of religion is, in its essence, a God-given right. In God's providence, our nation's Founders recognized this without debate and wove it into the fabric of the new nation's government. It appears both in the Declaration of Independence (where "Liberty" is listed as one of three "unalienable rights") and later in the U.S. Constitution (specifically, the First Amendment).

The original fall of man has produced an innate antipathy toward the living God. Consistent with that, America has devolved to a place where standing up for religious rights is now an increasing battleground in certain parts of the country. Too often, people cannot worship as they wish, without enduring the most detailed examination and evaluation of their basic beliefs or outright court battles. This is especially true for Christians, as ours is a religion of revelation based on moral absolutes. This irritates the natural mind with invigorated hatred of any standards claiming to be God-approved. What the Founders understood to be "self-evident" must now be fought for up to and including a Supreme Court ruling. Sadly, even the highest court in the nation often rules incorrectly.

It is difficult for many to comprehend how this 180-degree polar change came about from the Founders' very natural position of recognizing the Creator, to our modern U.S. government's sense of ownership of all liberty, which is to be doled out at the discretion of the State. A plausible explanation is that God sovereignly and specifically raised up the Founders and their fellow patriots from a biblically informed heritage and imparted to them a contempt for centralized government that would dare usurp the divine prerogatives of spiritual authority.

It is difficult for many to comprehend how this 180-degree polar change came about from the Founders' very natural position of recognizing the Creator, to our modern U.S. government's sense of ownership of all liberty.

Our spirits were created to worship God freely. Such worship cannot be coerced and should not be limited. But sadly, there is story after story, through biblical records and subsequent history, of governments using brutal means to force its citizens to confess belief in certain tenets and express devotion through ungodly rituals.

As early as the first generation after our Lord's resurrection and ascension into heaven, the fledgling churches of Galatia had been infiltrated by legalists who taught that the Jewish law of circumcision, along with faith in Christ, was essential to salvation. This distortion of the Gospel resulted in the Apostle Paul's fierce denunciation of such heresy and his affirmation of freedom, as stated in an early letter to the region:

"It is for freedom that Christ has set us free. Stand firm,

then, and do not let yourselves be burdened again by a yoke of slavery." (Gal. 5:1)

Our forefathers wrote the foundational documents for our nation with a completely different mindset than many so-called "progressives" have today. They were attempting to rid themselves of any state-sponsored religion. Even in the early days of the colonies, America, under British rule, had state-sponsored churches. But when independence from the Crown was established, the first new amendment of 10—and notice it was the very FIRST—began with this assertion:

"Congress shall make no law respecting an establishment of religion, or prohibiting the free exercise thereof."

Today's political climate is very different. The pendulum has swung in the other direction—from protecting religious expression to limiting freedom of expression. Today, our own government discourages and even persecutes those who are attempting to worship and follow the God of the Bible. Whether we look back a few hundred years or look at today, the focus is the same: freedom of worship. When religion is forced upon a populous by a government or is persecuted by a government, we need to pray for and protect our freedoms. God has created and granted this right, and many people in other parts of the world have paid the supreme sacrifice of martyrdom, simply because they would not renounce their faith or deny the truth of God's Word.

FREEDOMS COME FROM GOD

Freedom to worship whom we choose cannot be granted by human government. It can only be protected by a government or taken away. It exists because God created it. This is what our Founders believed, and this is what they stated and affirmed in the Declaration of Independence:

> "We hold these truths to be self-evident, that all men are created equal, that they are endowed by their Creator with certain unalienable Rights, that among these are Life, Liberty and the pursuit of Happiness."

The "unalienable Rights" include those rights within "Nature's Law" as our Founders put it. God created and imparted such principles. To go against these would be to go against the Creator's intention for proper freedom under a benevolent and protective government. Embedded deep within the Founders' minds and emotions was the conviction "to form a more perfect union" that created government and laws to reflect God's purpose.

This recognition of unalienable rights and Nature's Law is one of the primary reasons why our country has been so blessed. If we remove—or fail to recognize—that our country must continue to reflect the laws of God, then we are doomed as a nation.

Thomas Jefferson saw this from the beginning and noted the potential if not the inevitable decline, when he wrote, "The natural progress of things is for liberty to yield and government to gain ground."

The effectiveness of the Church becomes evident in a nation where there is freedom of religion. The Church was designed by God to be the thermostat of the nation. In the Sermon on the Mount, Jesus explained our purpose in this world:

> "You are the salt of the earth; but if the salt loses its flavor, how shall it be seasoned? It is then good for nothing but to

be thrown out and trampled underfoot by men. You are the light of the world. A city that is set on a hill cannot be hidden." (Mt. 5:13-14 NKJV)

If a nation begins to go down the wrong path in entertainment, education, government, civil rights, and the protection of the unborn, etc., we should not look for the crooked politician, the immoral entertainment leader, or the profiteering abortionist. Instead, we must first look at the Church for the origins of such deviations. What kind of influence—or lack of influence—are we having? The removal or persecution of religious freedoms will be one of the final steps in our nation's battle for morality. Without its protection, Christians will not be able to take the lead in creating legislation that reflects morality. In fact, persecution of Christian believers may well become rampant, even in the so-called "free world."

For decades, many American Christians have been comfortable, quietly taking our freedoms for granted, and not paying attention to the slow decay of all that God created for us to enjoy. Now, it is no longer comfortable to be a Christian in America. The world system may tolerate a Christian's belief in God's Word, but it is now in open warfare against a Christian's determination to "do God's Word"—i.e., to put those beliefs into action.

Much of this fight is turning local communities to activism in the form of the Religious Freedom Restoration Act (RFRA). RFRA laws date back to the 1990s, when this debate began to heat up. There have been many national iterations of the RFRA, with some having failed the support of our Supreme Court. But recently, a wave of wise state and local leaders have passed these types of laws to protect their people and the spiritual climate of their jurisdiction.

Many fear that total freedom of religion will permit Muslims,

Mormons, marijuana-smoking churches, and others to flourish. That fear is certainly valid, but to quote Bono (lead singer of U2), "Quit treating God like a little old lady crossing the street." If our God is the one living and true God, and we are an effective Church, we will not be intimidated by spiritual counterfeits. Where truth brings light to our communities, darkness will be overcome.

God's transforming Presence is sweeping through certain communities across the globe, supernaturally reviving His Church, and aligning governments with His law, allowing His people to worship freely. This occurs typically when a small group of intercessors gathers with humble hearts to seek Him and invite in His awesome Presence. Often He comes in such a manner that government authorities are inviting Christians to take on roles such as feeding the poor, ministering in jails, and leading other community initiatives. When the love and power of God are evident, even non-believing authorities soften toward the Lord, recognize the effectiveness of God's activity, and allow for the Church to be the Church.

PRAY THE BIBLE PROMISES THAT INSPIRED OUR FOUNDING FATHERS

The Prayer in the First Congress, A.D. 1774. Courtesy of the Rector, Church Wardens and Vestrymen of Christ Church, Philadelphia.

PRAYER POINTS:

DAY 1: Pray for the election of national, state, and local leaders who desire to protect freedom of religion.

DAY 1: Pray for leaders who understand that government should reflect the fear of God.

DAY 1: Pray for the Church to recognize its own critical state and need for renewal and revival.

DAY 1: Pray for Christian legal ministries that help believers stand for their freedoms under God.

DAY 1: Pray for a nationwide Great Awakening and Revival to stir the Church, bringing salvation to many, and extending God's kingdom rule.

✂ *Scriptures to Pray* ✂

- **PSALMS 33:12** – "Blessed is the nation whose God is the LORD . . ."
- **GALATIANS 5:1** – "It is for freedom that Christ has set us free. Stand firm, then, and do not let yourselves be burdened again by a yoke of slavery."
- **MATTHEW 5:13–14** – "You are the salt of the earth; but if the salt loses its flavor, how shall it be seasoned? It is then good for nothing but to be thrown out and trampled underfoot by men. You are the light of the world. A city that is set on a hill cannot be hidden" (NKJV).

CHAPTER EIGHT

GOD'S HEART FOR OUR NATION

"You are the light of the world.
A city that is set on a hill cannot be hidden."
(MATTHEW 5:14 NKJV)

One question remains: What is God's heart for our nation? We are bombarded by opinions and platforms of those who believe they know where to take our country, but where does God want to take our country? Our Founding Fathers had a strong sense that God not only formed this nation, but also had a specific destiny for it.

It was God who initiated in man the desire to explore and to establish societies in each new world. For example, He guided Christopher Columbus by way of the Scriptures and his natural observations. Contrary to popular myth, Columbus was not the first to think the earth was round. Much earlier records point to the writings of Aristotle and other Greek philosophers and mathematicians, as well as the Phoenicians.

Columbus's theories were influenced by Isa. 40:22, which says, "[God] sits enthroned above the circle of the earth." He also observed, as did others, that ships leaving the harbor "disappeared" from bottom to top as they sailed past the horizon and out of sight. With this confidence in the back of his mind, he wrote the King and Queen of Spain:

> "It was the Lord who put into my mind (I could feel his hand upon me) the fact that it would be possible to sail from here to the Indies. . . . I did not make use of intelligence, mathematics or maps. It is simply the fulfillment of what Isaiah had prophesied."

Later in his life, he journaled the importance of bringing the Gospel to this new world, motivated by the following two scriptures:

> "And this gospel of the kingdom will be preached in the whole world as a testimony to all nations, and then the end will come" (Mt. 24:14).

> "All the ends of the earth will remember and turn to the Lord, and all the families of the nations will bow down before him." (Ps. 22:27)

One of our nation's early governors, John Winthrop of Massachusetts, spoke eloquently when he said:

> "We are entered into Covenant with [God] for this work, we have taken out a commission if the Lord shall please to hear us and bring us in peace to the place we desire . . . [The people of New England must] follow the counsel of Micah, to do justly, to love mercy, to walk humbly with our God. For this end, we must be knit together in this work as one man, we must entertain each other in brotherly affection . . . we shall find that the God of Israel is among us, when tens of us shall be able to

resist a thousand of our enemies, when he shall make us a praise and a glory, that men shall say of succeeding plantations: the Lord make it like New England, for we must consider that we shall be as a City upon a Hill, the eyes of all people upon us."

George Washington's inaugural address is another example:

"No people can be bound to acknowledge and adore the Invisible Hand which conducts the affairs of men more than those of the United States. Every step by which they have advanced to the character of an independent nation seems to have been distinguished by some token of Providential Agency."

This "Providential Agency" has not only orchestrated past events, but also has within its scope God's future plans and purposes for nations. God establishes nations for His purposes: that the Gospel should go forth, both spoken and demonstrated.

"From one man [God] made all the nations, that they should inhabit the whole earth; and he marked out their appointed times in history and the boundaries of their lands. God did this so that they would seek him and perhaps reach out for him and find him, though he is not far from any one of us." (Acts 17:26-27)

This consideration of being a "city that is set on a hill" is in reference to Jesus' words in Mt. 5:14, where He called His disciples to be the light of the world and not to hide their lights under a basket. These men were the nucleus of the kingdom Jesus was introducing. They were the ones who, after His death and resurrection, would hear Him commission them to "go into all the world and preach the Gospel." They were the ones who would go forth after Pentecost, in the power of the Holy Spirit, to disciple nations. And they were successful, as the kingdom of God grew and Jesus Christ conquered by His love.

God establishes nations for His purposes: that the Gospel should go forth, both spoken and demonstrated.

It was the same Holy Spirit who led our forefathers to the New World to establish a God-fearing nation—indeed, a new city set on a new hill, yet preaching the "old, old story" of God's salvation through Christ. First, it was a few Pilgrims seeking religious freedom, then the Thirteen Colonies, filled with citizens (including our Founders) willing to risk everything to escape a monarchy that had become dictatorial. Finally, the "city" became the United States of America, a nation that would lead the world in the declaration of the Gospel, building peace, establishing righteousness, caring for fellow mankind, and becoming a haven for the tired and poor. It has always been the desire of God's heart that the Church's influence permeate society and be His active agent for doing good on the earth, for the benefit of all people.

God's plan, which the Founding Fathers understood, is for people to rely first on His providential care and second, on each other through work and honest commerce. Some think work was the result of Adam's fall, forcing people to earn "by the sweat of their brow," but Adam had work, keeping the Garden, before he and Eve fell to Satan's temptation.

EXCLUSIVE WORK OF THE CHURCH

As for charity, good works, caring for the sick and infirm, and rescuing babies from desertion and later from abortion, this was almost exclusively the work of the Church from the first century onward. It was God's people, not governments—repressive or generous—who built schools and hospitals, took in orphans, provided food for the hungry, and did countless other selfless good works. It was the kingdom of God in constant action.

U.S. President Calvin Coolidge (1923 to 1929) understood the importance of keeping government from being the nation's nursemaid and endless source of supply, which was also the Founders' intentions.[1] One year, he was asked to approve legislation sending $250,000 of relief aid to drought-stricken Texas, and in response, he wrote these wise words:

> "I can find no warrant for such an appropriation in the Constitution, and I do not believe that the power and duty of the general government ought to be extended to the relief of individual suffering. The lesson should constantly enforce that, though the people support the government, the government should not support the people. The friendliness and charity of our countryman can always be relied upon to relieve their fellow citizen in misfortune . . . Federal aid in such cases encourages the expectation of paternal care on the part of government and weakens the sturdiness of our national character, while it prevents the indulgence among our people of the kindly sentiment and conduct which strengthens the bonds of common brotherhood."

Our nation was founded upon God-given desires to provide for others, whether it was the Gospel, or justice, or righteousness—the entire gamut of activities that can be classified under our Lord's admonition to "love one another, as I have loved you" and "love your neighbor as yourself."

What is the heart of God for our nation? Our republic was established by God, and as a result our nation has been the favored "city on a hill" for more than two centuries. America has led the world in issues of righteousness and justice, while the Gospel was sent forth with finance and dedicated personnel unlike any other nation in the history of mankind. Led by an awakened and revived Church, may America rise again with a clear, unquenchable calling to become what our Lord and King desires us to be.

PRAY THE BIBLE PROMISES THAT INSPIRED OUR FOUNDING FATHERS

The Prayer in the First Congress, A.D. 1774. Courtesy of the Rector, Church Wardens and Vestrymen of Christ Church, Philadelphia.

PRAYER POINTS:

DAY 1: Give thanks and pray for elected officials who believe America has a divine origin and purpose.

DAY 2: Pray that in each national election, we will elect a Senate and House of Representatives who will insist, in their respective voting sessions, on a return to constitutional authority.

DAY 3: Pray that the Church would have a renewed sense of the government's role for our nation and the nation's role on the earth at this critical time in U.S. history.

DAY 4: Pray that our president, in God's mercy and providence, will restore the authority of the Constitution and all of its by laws.

DAY 5: Pray for any future presidential judiciary appointments, including vacancies that will arise on the U.S. Supreme Court.

✣ *Scriptures to Pray* ✣

- **MATTHEW 5:14** — "You are the light of the world. A city that is set on a hill cannot be hidden." (NKJV)
- **MATTHEW 24:14** — "And this gospel of the kingdom will be preached in the whole world as a testimony to all nations, and then the end will come."
- **ACTS 17:26-27** — "From one man [God] made all the nations, that they should inhabit the whole earth; and he marked out their appointed times in history and the boundaries of their lands. God did this so that they would seek him and perhaps reach out for him and find him, though he is not far from any one of us."

ENDNOTES:

[1]Calvin Coolidge, America's 30th president, held office from 1923 to 1929, having assumed the office from the vice-presidency upon the death of Warren G. Harding in 1923. Coolidge was known as a decisive leader and strict Constitutionalist. His integrity and respect for the law, including the balance of powers among the three branches of government, restored public confidence in the presidency that had been lost due to the Harding scandals. Americans have much to be thankful for in President Coolidge's tenure.

POSTSCRIPT

Most books conclude with the words "The End," but my goal is that these eight chapters on America's early history and the Founding Fathers' philosophy of government will be a launching pad, not a stopping point. I hope you share with me the positive outlook that it is not too late for our country to return to the godly ideals that made America so exceptional for nearly two centuries.

Sadly, those earlier days of domestic civil order and U.S. international leadership seem to have drifted away. Or were they "governed away" through carelessness and the imposition of beliefs that have taken our nation far from the U.S. Constitution? The Founders wanted a government that served and protected the people, while current political trends seem to be intent on increasing taxes and reducing personal freedoms.

Without wasting time casting blame, we believe this downward course can be turned around, as more and more Christians pray fervently and get involved in the voting process. Yes, we want to encourage a higher Christian voter turnout, but first, before we invest energy in "getting out the vote," we want to see an army of spiritual warriors join us in "getting out the prayer."

You have invested your valuable time to read and evaluate these chapters, so you no doubt share our belief that every election is the opportunity to recapture more of our nation's original values as we pray and vote for godly leaders. We believe that, as Christian men and women of faith, we must "always pray and not give up" (Lk. 18:1). We desperately need God's help, and He has promised in His Word to respond to the humble, repentant intercessors who call upon His name and seek His grace and mercy.

Calling Christians to intercede for elections and praying that God-fearing people will hold public office is not a new attempt to insert religion into the affairs of State. When the First Continental Congress convened in Philadelphia in 1774, the Rev. Jacob Duché, Rector of Christ Church, Philadelphia, was invited to Carpenters' Hall, to offer the initial opening prayer (see Chapter 5). This historic invocation is depicted graphically in every chapter just prior to our listed daily prayer points for each week, and is included here as a closing emphasis. And despite ongoing, desperate attempts by secular individuals and agencies to oust religion from government, both the House and the Senate maintain chaplains who offer daily prayers when the U.S. Congress is in session.

PRAY THE BIBLE PROMISES THAT INSPIRED OUR FOUNDING FATHERS

The Prayer in the First Congress, A.D. 1774. Courtesy of the Rector,
Church Wardens and Vestrymen of Christ Church, Philadelphia.

AN ACTION STEP

If this historical review represents your heart, please look closely at the various opportunities Intercessors for America has made available to coordinate a national prayer initiative. You can start by visiting ifapray. org and responding as you are led. Be encouraged! God's people are awakening, and His Church is on the move!

The Prayer in the First Congress

O Lord our Heavenly Father, high and mighty King of kings, and Lord of lords, who dost from thy throne behold all the dwellers on earth and reignest with power supreme and uncontrolled over all the Kingdoms, Empires and Governments; look down in mercy, we beseech Thee, on these our American States, who have fled to Thee from the rod of the oppressor and thrown themselves on Thy gracious protection, desiring to be henceforth dependent only on Thee. To Thee have they appealed for the righteousness of their cause; to Thee do they now look up for that countenance and support, which Thou alone canst give. Take them, therefore, Heavenly Father, under Thy nurturing care; give them wisdom in Council and valor in the field; defeat the malicious designs of our cruel adversaries; convince them of the unrighteousness of their Cause and if they persist in their sanguinary purposes, of own unerring justice, sounding in their hearts, constrain them to drop the weapons of war from their unnerved hands in the day of battle!

Be Thou present, O God of wisdom, and direct the councils of this honorable assembly; enable them to settle things on the best and surest foundation. That the scene of blood may be speedily closed; that order, harmony and peace may be effectually restored, and truth and justice, religion and piety, prevail and flourish amongst the people. Preserve the health of their bodies and vigor of their minds; shower down on them and the millions they here represent, such temporal blessings as Thou seest expedient for them in this world and crown them with everlasting glory in the world to come. All this we ask in the name and through the merits of Jesus Christ, Thy Son and our Savior.

Amen.

Reverend Jacob Duché
Rector of Christ Church of Philadelphia, Pennsylvania
September 7, 1774, 9 a.m.

PRAY THE NAMES OF JESUS OVER OUR NATION

". . . that at the name of Jesus every knee should bow"
(PHILIPPIANS 2:10)

This guide provides a Name of Jesus, each with a Scripture reference, organized by letters of the alphabet. We encourage you to look up the references and pray the names and verses of Scripture over our nation, as the Lord leads you.

A

Adam, the Second – 1 Cor. 15:45-47
Advocate – 1 Jn. 2:1
Almighty – Rev. 1:8
Alpha and Omega – Rev. 21:6
Amen – Rev. 3:14
Ancient of Days – Dan. 7:9
Angel, Mine – Ex. 23:20-23
Angel of His Presence – Isa. 63:9
Anointed Above His Fellows – Ps. 45:7
Anointed, His – Ps. 2:2

Apostle of Our Profession – Heb. 3:1
Arm of the Lord – Isa. 51:9-10
Author and Finisher of Our Faith – Heb. 12:2
Author of Eternal Salvation – Heb. 5:9

B

Begotten of God – 1 Jn. 5:18
Beloved – Eph. 1:6
Bishop of Souls – 1 Pet. 2:25
Blessed and Only Potentate – 1 Tim. 6:15
Branch, A Righteous – Jer. 23:5
Branch of Righteousness – Jer. 33:15
Branch of the Root of Jesse – Isa. 11:1
Branch – Zech. 3:8
Bread of Life – Jn. 6:35
Bright and Morning Star – Rev. 22:16

C

Captain of the Lord's Host – Josh. 5:15
Carpenter's Son – Mt. 13:55
Chief Cornerstone – 1 Pet. 2:6
Chiefest among Ten Thousand – S. of S. 5:10
Christ, The – Jn. 1:41
Christ the Lord – Lk. 2:11
Christ Jesus Our Lord – Rom. 8:39
Christ the Power of God – 1 Cor. 1:24
Counselor – Isa. 9:6
Covenant of the People – Isa. 42:6

D

Dayspring – Lk. 1:78
Day Star – 2 Pet. 1:19
Deliverer – Rom. 11:26
Door, The – Jn. 10:7-10

E

Elect – Isa. 42:1
Emmanuel – Mt. 1:23
Eternal Life – 1 Jn. 5:20
Everlasting Father – Isa. 9:6

F

Faithful and True – Rev. 19:11
Faithful Witness – Rev. 1:5
Firstbegotten – Heb. 1:6
Firstborn – Ps. 89:27
Firstborn among Many Brethren – Rom. 8:29
First and Last – Rev. 22:13
Firstfruits – 1 Cor. 15:23
Foundation Laid in Zion – Isa. 28:16

G

Glorious Lord –Isa. 33:21
God of Israel – Isa. 45:15
God with Us – Mt. 1:23
Good Shepherd – Jn. 10:11
Great God – Titus 2:13
Great High Priest – Heb.4:14

H

Head of the Body – Col. 1:18
Head over All Things – Eph. 1:22
Head Stone of the Corner– Ps. 118:22
Heir of All Things – Heb. 1:2
Holy One of Israel – Isa. 41:14
Hope of Glory – Col. 1:27
Horn of Salvation – Lk. 1:69

I

I Am – Jn. 8:58
Image of the Invisible God – Col.1:15
Immanuel – Isa. 7:14

J

Jesus Christ Our Lord – Rom. 1:3
Jesus of Nazareth – Acts 22:8
Judge of Israel – Mic. 5:1

K

King – Zech. 9:9
King of Glory – Ps. 24:7
King of Kings – Rev. 17:14
King of the Jews – Mk. 15:2
King over All the Earth – Zech.14:9

L

Lamb of God – Jn. 1:29
Life – Jn. 14:6
Light of the World – Jn. 8:12
Lily of the Valleys – S. of S. 2:1
Lion of Judah – Rev. 5:5
Living Bread – Jn. 6:51
Lord and Savior – 2 Pet. 2:20
Lord God Almighty – Rev. 4:8
Lord of All – Acts 10:36
Lord Our Righteousness – Jer. 23:6
Lord, Your Redeemer – Isa. 43:14
Love – 1 Jn.4:8

M

Man of Sorrows – Isa. 53:3

Master – Mt. 23:10
Mediator – 1 Tim. 2:5
Messiah – Dan. 9:25
Mighty God – Isa. 9:6
Mighty One of Jacob – Isa. 60:16
Morning Star – Rev. 2:28
Most Holy – Dan. 9:24
Most Mighty – Ps. 45:3

N

Nazarene – Mt. 2:23

O

Only Begotten Son – Jn. 3:16
Only Wise God – 1 Tim. 1:17
Our Passover – 1 Cor. 5:7

P

Physician – Lk. 4:23
Prince of Peace – Isa. 9:6
Prince of the Kings of the Earth – Rev. 1:5
Prophet – Deut. 18:15-18
Propitiation – Rom. 3:25

R

Rabbi – Jn. 1:49
Redeemer – Isa. 59:20
Resurrection – Jn. 11:25
Righteous Servant – Isa. 53:11
Rock – 1 Cor. 10:4
Root of Jesse – Isa. 11:10
Rose of Sharon – S. of S. 2:1

S

Savior of the World – 1 Jn. 4:14
Seed of David – Jn. 7:42
Seed of the Woman – Gen. 3:15
Son of Abraham – Mt. 1:1
Son of David – Mt. 1:1
Son of God – Rom. 1:4
Son of Man – Acts 7:56
Son of Mary – Mk. 6:3
Son of the Highest – Lk. 1:32
Star out of Jacob – Num. 24:17
Stone – Mt. 21:42
Strong Tower – Ps. 61:3
Sun of Righteousness – Mal. 4:2
Sure Foundation – Isa. 28:16

T

Teacher – Jn. 3:2
Tried Stone – Isa. 28:16
Truth – Jn. 14:6

U

Unspeakable Gift – 2 Cor. 9:15
Upholder of All Things – Heb. 1:3

V

Vine – Jn. 15:1

W

Way – Jn. 14:6
Wisdom – Prov. 8:12, 1 Cor. 1:24
Wonderful – Isa. 9:6
Word – Jn. 1:14
Word of God – Rev. 19:13
Word of Life – 1 Jn. 1:1